Celtic Spirituality

Rhythm, Roots and Relationships

Ray Simpson

Guardian, Community of Aidan and Hilda, Lindisfarne

GROVE BOOKS LIMITED
RIDLEY HALL RD CAMBRIDGE CB3 9HU

Contents

1   An Overview of Celtic Christian Spirituality 3

2   The Power of Place 9

3   The Value of Soul Friendship 17

Resources for the Practical Application of the Themes of This Book 26

Notes 27

The Cover Illustration is by Peter Ashton
and is based on an eagle from the Book of Kells

Copyright © Ray Simpson 2003

First Impression May 2003
ISSN 0262-799X
ISBN 1 85174 530 0

An Overview of Celtic Christian Spirituality

1

Throughout history great movements of spirituality have risen up. They bring light into new or neglected areas of human life.

They reconnect believers with the sources of their faith, and they connect these with the contemporary world. The Celtic renewal does this for a world that is drained and fragmented after centuries of materialism, rationalism and dehumanizing forms of hierarchy.

Oliver Davies, in his volume on *Celtic Spirituality* in *The Classics of Western Spirituality* writes:

> There is something peculiarly attractive about the Christianity of the early Celtic-speaking peoples, which continues to exercise a considerable fascination on many today…God was present to them in images and signs, in poetry and art, in sacrament and liturgy; and their own response to God was no less direct, for it was commonly a physical one, expressed at the level of the body in the embrace of a life-transforming penance. Indeed, it is these two themes, penance and creativity, that are the guiding motifs of Celtic Christianity. Both speak of incarnation, and of the affirmation and transformation of life, since creativity is the mark of the Spirit and penance is the gate of glory.[1]

Celtic-style Christians see life as a pilgrimage. Ian Bradley draws out these characteristics of the tradition of St Columba:[2]

- Devotion based on prayer, psalms and poetry
- Theology based on the praise, protection and presence of God
- Churches that are provisional, penitent and on pilgrimage.

Celtic spirituality is marked by the belief that what is deepest in us is the image of God. Sin has distorted and obscured that image but has not erased it. Philip Newell contrasts this belief with the Mediterranean tradition which, on the other hand, 'in its doctrine of original sin has taught that what is deepest in us is our sinfulness. This has given rise to a tendency to define ourselves in terms of the ugliness of our failings instead of the beauty of our origins.'[3]

Unlike in some creation theology, however, sin is taken seriously. Ceaseless war is waged against evil in both the human and the spirit world. Memorizing Scripture, praying daily in the rhythm of the sun, and working with a soul friend to overcome destructive passions are a means to this.

The early Celtic churches were communities of work, prayer and hospitality at the heart of local life

Celtic Christian spirituality is Bible-centred. Scripture was constantly repeated and reflected upon. St Patrick (fifth century) has 340 quotations from 46 books of the Bible in his two short writings.

The early Celtic churches were communities of work, prayer and hospitality at the heart of local life, and Christians with a Celtic vision seek to restore these features to church life today.

In the Celtic tradition there is no real divide between this world and the other world. God is close at hand, and so are the saints and angels, who can be talked to in the most familiar terms.

David Adam in *The Eye of the Eagle* suggests:

> The Celtic vision derives much of its insight from St John's gospel, and the symbol of that gospel is the eagle…The eagle's vision was able to look deeper and see beyond others, to see what for others was invisible…The Celtic church in its love for St John's Gospel sought to have this vision. They prayed that their eyes might be opened, that all their senses might be made alert to that which was invisible. They prayed that they might have the eagle's eyes to see him who comes at all times.[4]

In one sense the Celtic Christian tradition is simply natural, orthodox Christianity. Members of churches in Celtic lands between the fifth and eleventh centuries would have thought of themselves as part of the one, undivided church, faithful to the teaching of Christ and the apostles and to their contemporary successors.

However, over time that natural, orthodox Christianity has been overlaid and fragmented. Celtic spirituality seeks simplicity and that inner fire which naturally purifies, and therefore does not enforce allegiance through unwieldy regulation and edifice.

The vivid sense of the Trinity which marks Celtic spirituality is certainly not unique to it, but, as Athanasius pointed out, it was the church in Celtic lands that remained true to the Trinity during the fourth century Arian controversy. Celtic poetry reveals not just belief in, but love of the Trinity. The Western Church has largely lost that love, and has detached Christ from the Trinity.

Being on the Edge

Celtic spirituality today recognizes that the great threads which made up the cloth of early Christianity have become separated. Many see in it a way to weave together again the Catholic, Evangelical, Pentecostal, Orthodox and Radical strands, and to heal a fragmented world.

When I announced I was to move to Lindisfarne, a newly appointed archdeacon warned 'Whatever you do, keep this Celtic renewal on the edges. If they succeed in moving it from the edge to the middle they will kill it.' People have attempted to 'cage the eagle' both historically and today.

The Western Church has largely lost that love, and has detached Christ from the Trinity

Celts emerged from Europe's heartlands but the Roman troops pushed them to the western fringes of Britain, Ireland and Gaul (France). Celtic Christians believe God takes us to the edges of life. Jesus allowed himself to be pushed to the edges of society. That is why he could communicate to so many ordinary people. Often it is only when we are willing to go to edges that we truly meet others, for many who are on edges of loneliness, anger, despair or adventure recognize and reach out to another who is on an edge. This is how the truly precious things of life are passed on—at the edges. And at the edge we see horizons denied to those who stay where they are comfortable. We are called to mould the kingdoms of the earth so that they reflect the kingdom of heaven. The edge is in fact always the centre of spiritual renewal.

The Benedictine Rule replaced the various Celtic Rules during the eighth and succeeding centuries. Without doubt it was necessary to moderate some of the extreme asceticism of the latter, and to create more moderate, stable communities. Yet with the imposition of standardized Rules throughout the Western Church some things were lost—the flame of passion, the freedom to wander at the impulse of the Spirit, the ability to explore wild places within and without us. The Eastern Church has retained the flexibility and local character of each monastery, and has enabled individual callings and extreme acts of devotion to flourish under one umbrella.

At the edge we see horizons denied to those who stay where they are comfortable

The Celtic model for Christianizing peoples is not to impose, but to invite. It does so with such love and vulnerability that every part of society and every part of an individual's psyche chooses to embrace Christ and experiences real conversion. Of course, this ideal was often not attained, but it was—notably in the first pioneer period—wholeheartedly pursued, and is now being pursued again.

In the second millennium both society and church became fragmented and blindly individualistic. The most significant new development in human society is the rapid expansion of possibilities for human interconnectedness. Former United States President Bill Clinton pointed out that when he became President in 1993 there were just 50 sites on the worldwide web. When he left office in 2002 there were 350 million sites. Celtic spirituality enables us to live in the awareness of our interconnectedness with both humans and all that lives. In Celtic art, the unbroken thread that runs through even the most intricate of patterns is a symbol of this truth.

Celtic spirituality enables us to live in the awareness of our interconnectedness

In an age of instant communication it is possible to let a thousand flowers bloom and still maintain cohesion. We have more opportunity to foster both these strands and we have no need to emasculate either of them.

Returning to Roots

The purpose of the Way of Life of The Community of Aidan and Hilda, of which I am Guardian, is to broaden and deepen our experience of Christianity. Too many expressions of Christianity have embraced developments that came after the major splits in the universal church (11th century and 15th century) but have excluded expressions of that deeper, unfissured spirituality of the Desert, of the Eastern fathers and Celtic saints. We seek to restore this to its crucial place in our Christian birthright, as well as to draw on great flowerings of spirituality in other periods. Celtic Christianity is a celebration of the roots of our faith.

We have more opportunity to foster both these strands and we have no need to emasculate either of th

Celtic spirituality is often romanticized. Pagan, as well as Christian Celtic spirituality is undergoing a revival with earth energies, channelled spirits, and 'the goddess within' becoming substitutes for the true God. Few of the romanticizers want to know about deliverance from evil spirits, penance, fasting and vigil, which are integral to the Christian Celtic tradition.

Within the Christian fold, some people romanticize the period of the early Celtic church as a Golden Age, and use the label 'Celtic' for anything that seems creative. Scholars debate the degree to which there is a valid connection between the church in Celtic lands in the period 400–700 and the smorgasbord of spiritualities which claim the label 'Celtic' today. Documents are fragmentary, much is not certain, each region was distinctive, and opportunities for mass education, communication and creative arts were more limited. This does not invalidate the use of the term 'Celtic' as a symbol for today. For symbols accrue energies, and some key features of the early church in Celtic lands have become symbols which now bear their own life.

Celtic Christian spirituality eschews romantic and pagan imaginings which are not compatible with Christian and human realities. It is rooted in the orthodox, Trinitarian Faith which the early church in Celtic lands adhered to so wholeheartedly. And it embraces and integrates authentic contemporary expressions of spirituality which are regarded to be in some sense 'Celtic' because of their feel, rather than because of documentary analysis. The *'three R's'* have been used to describe modern Celtic style churches. They focus on *roots* in the land, *rapport* with the people and *rhythm* with God.

We draw inspiration from them in order that Christianity may be lived naturally

We do not seek to copy Celtic Christians or to focus on them for their own sake. We draw inspiration from them in order that Christianity may be lived naturally, in organic continuity with its roots, thus recovering wholeness. We seek to reconnect with this previously neglected part of our birthright in order to journey on to new places of resurrection. We seek to re-sacralize the world, to recover a way of seeing the world as an expression of the Creator, and to make it holy. Celtic spirituality crosses frontiers. It goes so deep that, without losing what is distinctive, it becomes universal. Our Rule can be applied by people of any nationality.

The movements God has raised up at different times in Christian history share common features, but each also has a distinctive calling. Attempts have been made to encapsulate the great movements in one word: Poverty (Franciscans); Obedience (Jesuits); Stability (Benedictines); Unity (Focolare); Peace (Bruderhof). What word best encapsulates the Celtic renewal? I tentatively suggest 'Rhythm.' The Celtic renewal helps us to re-connect with God as revealed in the primal rhythms of creation, the soul and the church year.

In his book *Celtic Christianity: Making Myths and Chasing Dreams*,[5] Ian Bradley gives an overview of six waves of Celtic spirituality through history. I believe that the current Celtic renewal will be more far reaching than the previous four, and certainly than the Victorian 'Celtic Twilight' movement associated with the revival of Romanticism and 'nature' poets such as Wordsworth and Ruskin. The current renewal is coterminous with the most significant change in society and the church since the Constantinian revolution of the fourth century.

Questions for Reflection

1 Trying to fit people into a 'one shape fits all' church does not work today, yet there is a 'control freak' tendency inside most of us. If contemplation is the antidote to control, how assiduously are we practising contemplation?

2 If life-transforming penance and creativity are the two main motifs of Celtic spirituality, as Oliver Davies suggests, how do we embrace a true repentance of heart that makes us feel sorrow (2 Corinthians 7.9) and tap into the creative wellspring within us?

3 If rediscovering God-intended primal rhythms is vital, how can I reflect the rhythm of the sun's rising and setting in daily prayer?

The Power of Place 2

Christianity abhors idolatry, and places can become idols.

Jesus warned a Samaritan of this danger when he explained that neither her special place (a mountain) nor the Jews' special place (Jerusalem) would be the focus for worship, which could be anywhere, since 'God is Spirit and truth' (John 4.21–24).

The Celtic Christian understanding of place derives precisely from the acknowledgement of the presence of the Spirit in every part of the earth, in every facet of life, and in the process of discernment as to where a Christian or a venture of faith should be, and how it should relate to its environment.

The Celtic Christian tradition understands that the divine nature (which is to draw all into co-unity) is perceived in the things God has created (Romans 1.20). God uses natural elements to draw people into harmony with each other and with God. Each place has its distinctive arrangement of these elements. For example, secluded, fertile valleys draw people because they offer both shelter and life-sustaining water. High places draw people because they offer a vantage point which imparts safety and authority. These physical attributes have psychic and spiritual dimensions. Such places are holy in the sense that they provide peace, beauty, perspective, or evoke an awareness of the transcendent.

Each feature of these places may reveal to us something about God's nature

There is nothing specifically Christian about these. However, prayers in the Celtic Christian tradition, such as *St Patrick's Breastplate*, call on the elements to bless and protect human beings, knowing that there is already something holy and powerful present in these elements when they are invited to be in harmony with their Creator's purposes. So when we come to a place of peace, beauty or special memory, we may call on the various physical features in that place to bless the Lord, on the lines of Psalm 148. Each feature of these places may reveal to us something about God's nature.

Certain places are holy because their different parts fit well together to make a whole. Good planning and inspired architecture can provide an urban backdrop as inspiring in its way as is a beautiful landscape. When the different groups, services and institutions in a place relate well together and have a unified focus (that is to say, they are not a law unto themselves) then there is a measure of 'shalom' in that place.

There are places 'on the edge' which may be as different as a rocky peninsula or a poverty-stricken slum, which a godly person has made holy in spite of a hostile environment. The Bible gives many examples of God declaring a place holy because a person has made covenant with God there. After Moses' divine encounter near a burning desert bush God declared this to be holy ground (Exodus 3.5). Sinai, where Moses communed with God, was known as the holy mountain (Exodus 18.5). The areas around which holy people lived became hallowed places. Many a town or city takes its name from a Christian who first lived there, and drew round them others for whom prayer was work and work was prayer.

The Holy Place

> The life and passion of a person leaves an imprint on the ether of a place.
> Love does not remain within the heart,
> it flows out to build secret tabernacles in the landscape.
>
> John O'Donohue[6]

The holy place, which is a meeting place with God, is a recurring theme in Scripture. Each of the patriarchs set up altars in places where God had met with them in a special way. These were usually made of stone. Names were given to these places which reflected the experience that had taken place; for example, Bethel (House of God), so named by Jacob after his vision of God there (Genesis 28.11–22).

Jesus had special meeting places with God Jesus had special meeting places with God, sometimes in the desert, at other times on a mountainside. The Celtic Christians had special places in the rocky peninsulas or forests that served as deserts for them. Place names like Dysart, Disert, Diarmada, Desertoghill still recall what once were numinous places for solitaries.

Jesus also had special places of meeting with God's friends. He told his disciples that after his resurrection he would go to Galilee and they were to meet him there (Matthew 26.32; 28.10, 16).

At the root of the idea of holy places is the incarnation of God in a particular person, in a particular place, at a particular time. This principle does not only apply to the supreme point in history—the first Easter in Jerusalem—it applies at points throughout history. So if an apostle plants a work of God in a place, it becomes a little Jerusalem. There are Jerusalems, Nazareths, Galilees and Bethlehems in every land. Bethlehem is holy because in the simplicity of smelly straw the most holy person was born of a faith-filled mother and saluted by angels. Galilee is holy because its lake, mountains, spaces and beauty drew holy people to it, who then drew crowds. Nazareth is an image of a place hidden from public view where spiritual formation is taking place. Jerusalem is meant to be an image of a city, each of whose parts is perfectly joined together in unity (Psalm 122) even though, before and since Christ's presence there, it has become the centre of religious empire builders and a place of strife.

In the fourth century Christian Europe came to be dotted with shrines of holy people and martyrs where, people sensed, heaven and earth met. The shrines, containing a grave or just a fragment of a saint's bones, were often quite simply called 'the place.' Gildas, writing of the Roman Emperor Diocletian's persecution of Christians, observed that 'God lit for us the brilliant lamps of holy martyrs. Their graves and the places where they suffered would now have the greatest effect in instilling the blaze of divine love in the minds of onlookers.'[7] Bede records that Germanus, Bishop of Auxerre, took away with him a portion of earth from the place where the martyr Alban's blood had been shed.[8]

The saintly seventh century King Oswald and his soldiers knelt in a field where a battle with the tyrant invader was to take place, and planted a cross of wood in its earth. They won the battle, and Oswald named that place Heavenfield. That spot marked a turning point in the destiny of the British Isles, it was the scene of innumerable miracles, and moss scraped from the surface of the Cross proved potent to heal disease.

> For the blood of thy martyrs and saints
> Shall enrich the earth, shall create holy places.
> For wherever a saint has dwelt, wherever a martyr has given his blood
>   for the blood of Christ,
> There is holy ground, and the sanctity shall not depart from it
> Though armies trample over it, though sightseers come with
>   guidebooks looking over it;
> From where the western seas gnaw at the coast of Iona,
> To the death in the desert, the prayer in forgotten places by the broken
>   imperial column,
> From such ground springs that which forever renews the earth
> Though it is for ever denied.
>   T S Eliot, *Murder in the Cathedral*[9]

A holy place evokes an atmosphere of devotion, invites prayer and carries a story. It can be a means of mission. It inspires encounters with God. 'New' places can be hallowed. When the astronaut Neil Armstrong reached the moon he placed upon it a celluloid copy of the Genesis account of God creating the world. He was hallowing the moon.

Each place, like each person, has its own God-given charism or potential. The aim of the believer should be to release the place to be its true self, not to copy other places. In the Celtic tradition God is also in the middle of every-day life—the home, the job, the playground. These too, are holy ground.

God Leads People to the Right Place

The lives of Celtic saints abound with examples of the Holy Spirit guiding the saint to the place he wishes them to live, often to found a faith commu-nity. The components of divine guidance in these stories include the inward witness of the Spirit, the trail of a friendly wild creature, the sensing of crea-tion's friendship, the invitation of a land owner, the spirit of the local people and prophecy.

Mungo was led by a wild stag to found a community at what is now Llanelwy. Patrick changed his own mission itinerary in order to bless a plain where a good pagan welcomed him and became a believer. David of Wales changed his intention to found a monastic village in a certain place, because God revealed to him that only a small percentage of its population would go to heaven, whereas in another place (now St David's) many would go to heaven.

The Lives of Celtic saints abound with examples of the Holy Spirit guiding the saint to the place he wishes them to live

Ciaran, son of a carpenter, went to the Isle of Aran to be mentored by that great teacher of the spiritual life, Enda. Once, as they com-muned in prayer, they both received the same vision. A great and fruitful tree stood beside a river in the centre of Ireland. The tree protected the entire island, its fruit was taken across the sea, and birds of the world carried off other fruit. The interpretation was given to Enda. The tree was Ciaran. All Ireland would be covered by the grace that God had put within him. God was sending him to found a faith community on the banks of a river in the middle of Ireland. Many people would be nourished through the fasting and prayer.

It was some years, and after 'trial and error,' before Ciaran was led to the place that, with hindsight, was seen as the fulfilment of the vision. First he went to some brothers near Lake Isel. There, a nearby settlement of hooli-gans disturbed the brothers. After Ciaran's dedicated prayer the situation changed. But some of the brothers became jealous of the graces God bestowed on Ciaran, so he departed with some brothers for Inis Angin. At first this did not look a propitious place. The harbour was deserted except for a loud mouthed heathen youth. Ciaran urged his brothers to befriend him, and prophesied that one day that youth would be his abbot. Ciaran became his mentor and he indeed succeeded Ciaran as abbot at the place he was led to next. After three years and three months on Inis Angin, Ciaran came to a place on the banks of the river Shannon. Was this the place of the prophecy? When he saw its beauty he said: 'If we stay here we will have plenty of this world's wealth but few souls will go to heaven.' So he moved to a place known as 'Height of the Well.' In this place, Ciaran discerned, there would be communion with God. So he and eight companions set up their monastery at Clonmacnoise. Ciaran died, probably of the plague, less than a year after establishing this community. Yet it flourished for a thousand years, and today thousands still go to pray in its fine remains. Columba, the great Irish saint who later founded the Iona family of monasteries, took a container of earth from Clonmacnoise. He believed that if it was sprinkled on a piece of land God would make that spot fruitful.

In this place, Ciara discerned, there would be communion with God

There are no slick short cuts to discernment. What does one make of the story from the *Book of Lismore* of a formidable woman named Canair who had a vision of a tower of fire rising from every faith community in Ireland, but the tallest and straightest towards heaven of these towers arose from an island called Inis Cathaig. 'I must leave here, and go and live there,' Canair decided, 'for that will be the place of my resurrection.'

Unfortunately for her, the hermit Senan, who already lived there, was equally formidable, and the presence of a woman on the island he had made his own was not part of his vision. Senan welcomed her at the harbour, but suggested she travel on to her sister some miles away. 'I have not come here in order to do that,' Canair retorted, 'I have come here to stay with you on this island. Christ came to redeem women no less than men. Women have always tended and served Christ and his apostles. So why can't you receive women on your island?' 'You are stubborn,' Senan told her. 'In that case shall I get what I ask for—a place for myself on this island and to receive the Sacrament from you?'

'You will be given your place of resurrection,' said Senan, 'but it will be here on the sea's edge; and I fear the sea will carry off your remains.' 'The spot of earth on which my dead body shall lie will not be the first spot of earth that this sea will carry away' the woman asserted.

Who had the last word? Canair had hardly noticed that while they had been debating, the sea had come up to her waist. So they had to move a little up the shore, where Senan did give her Holy Communion. And, according to this account, Canair went straight to heaven.[10]

The Place of Resurrection

The idea that we each have a place of resurrection was prevalent in the stories of Irish saints, though the concept is not explained. Two things are clear. First, people need to keep moving with God until they find their place of resurrection. Some students asked Molaise of Ferns, who was a prominent soul friend, to help them discern where was their place of resurrection. He took them to a hill and pointed them in several directions. 'Did you hear a bell ring when you looked at any of these places?' he asked them. None rang a bell with them. So Molaise advised them that their place of resurrection must be beyond the horizon. This story has prompted advice I sometimes give: 'Let your feet follow your heart until you find your place of resurrection.'

Let your feet follow your heart until you find your place of resurrection

Secondly, it is clear that these early Irish believed that the spirit of the deceased Christian would continue to be used by God in that place of their primary calling. It was therefore considered to be important that they were buried in that place. The aged Brendan died in the arms of his sister Brig at her place. Before he died he insisted that they take his corpse to his place of resurrection. That was Clonfert, where he had painstakingly built up a faith community of several thousands and had written its rule of life. The work they would do there after their death was intercession for the people of that place. Thus Moninna (also known as Darerca) who founded the faith community at Killeevy, in Armagh, told the grieving locals as they gathered round her death bed: 'Do not be sad at my leaving you. For I truly believe that Christ, with whom I now go to stay, will give you whatever I ask of him in heaven no less than when I prayed to him on earth.'[11]

God Calls People to Hallow Places

Aidan of Lindisfarne, apostle to the English, taught his students to pray and fast in a place for 40 days before beginning to build anything. A Northumbrian king asked Aidan's former student Cedd, Bishop of the East Saxons, to build a monastery on uninhabited land where the king might come to pray, learn and be buried. Bede records that Cedd chose a site amid steep and rugged hills which seemed better fitted for the haunts of thieves and wild beasts than for humans, so that, as Isaiah says 'Where once dragons were shall be grass with reeds and rushes' (Isaiah 35.7, AV). Bede explains 'that is, the fruit of good works shall spring up where once beasts dwelt or where men lived after the manner of beasts.'[12]

Cedd was anxious first to cleanse the site from the stain of former crimes by prayer and fasting, before laying the foundations. So he gained the king's permission to spend the whole of Lent there in prayer.

Reclaiming Sacred Space

> Landscape has a secret and silent memory,
> a narrative of presence
> where nothing is ever lost or forgotten.
>
> John O'Donohue[13]

Some so-called holy places are really religious places where 'empire building' has a heyday. The holiness and the wholeness which once marked truly hallowed places can be frittered away or overlaid with money, malice or mindless pleasure. The holy places can be destroyed unless the people who live in them get in line with God, as God made clear to the prophet Amos (Amos 7.7–9). In Britain, the harmony and unity of the old culture were destroyed by the invading Normans, the nation was divided into master and serf, and the land was trodden under. Yet the original hallowing is still buried there, waiting to be re-discovered, and re-connected with the present. Today people who sense the aura of places are being drawn to sing, play music, prayer walk or dance in them. Some Christians are called to re-awaken prayer and 'Presence' in ancient holy places.

The holy places can be destroyed unless the people who live in them get in line with God

The mystery of who God is is released into the landscape, which reveals its secrets bit by bit to those who wait, are still, and reflect. To relate in a healing way to the landscape requires reciprocity. The Eskimos, when they kill a seal for their use, pour water back into it. They understand reciprocity.

The value of 'Sacred Space' is increasingly being recognized. Even if we live in a country without a long Christian history, we can tap into a hallowing process, which is at a different stage in each land.

Healing the Earth

This requires us to relate to the earth as partners, not oppressors. We need to cherish it, give it rest, respect its nature and its rhythms and to bless it. Rest is part of the healing of the earth. The majority of farming in the western world is now driven by money. Soil that should have a time for rest, when insects, wild plants and the recuperative powers of nature can have their day, is now poisoned in order for the land to be operative throughout the year. Celtic monastic churches kept the Sabbath (Saturday) special, as well as Sunday. These were both days for praying, eating and relaxing together. The land and the animals were given a rest too.

In chapter four of his *Life of Ninian*, Aelred reports that as a result of the local ruler being hard and hostile towards the man who was bringing in God's kingdom 'the soil seemed rejected and nearest to an accursed thing, since as it drank the rain falling upon it, it produced thorns and thistles instead of wholesome plants.' This can be contrasted with Aelred's story in chapter seven, of vegetables sprouting out of season in the monastery grounds, as a result of the prayer of faith.[14]

Healing the earth is explored more fully in Volume Three of my *Celtic Prayer Book*.[15]

Questions for Reflection

1   If God manifests his presence in the elements, become aware of the elements that shape the place where you are. What attributes of God do you sense are present or missing?

2   Which, as far as you are aware, is the nearest place to you that has been formed by a holy person?

    What in it calls out for prayer, repentance or celebration?

3   What in your parish or community seems to be a 'no-go area' for God? What needs to be reclaimed, and how could you go about doing this?

The Value of Soul Friendship 3

The early Celtic Christians knew that the soul, to know itself, must be known by another.

Heart must speak to heart. Even Jesus, who wholly embraced his friendship with his divine Father, needed human friends because he was also fully human. He chose three to be with him at significant moments. Of these three, John seems to have had greatest understanding. John thought of himself as the disciple whom Jesus loved. It was John to whom Jesus bequeathed the care of his mother, and *vice versa*. Celtic believers have always had a deep rapport with John as the contemplative who entered into heart communion with Jesus.

Like the desert fathers and mothers, Celtic Christians knew that to understand oneself one must be able to pour out the thoughts of the heart to another. The central importance of this is illustrated by the popular saying, linked with the fifth century Brigid and the eighth century *Celi De* ('Friends of God') reform movement, that a person without a soul friend was like a body without a head. For in that society it was believed that the soul resided in the head.

> *They knew that to understand oneself one must be able to pour out the thoughts of the heart to another*

Our knowledge of the development of soul friendship in the church in Celtic lands comes from three main sources—the desert Christians, the various *Lives* of the Celtic saints, and the spiritual disciplines inculcated in *The Penitentials*.[16]

The Desert Christians

Three formative fifth century faith communities in Gaul were those at Tours (established by Martin), Lerins (founded by Honoratus) and Marseilles (Cassian). Cassian had spent a year with the desert Christians and, through his writings about them, influenced the development of soul friendship in Britain and Ireland, where his writings circulated.

A key lesson Cassian learned from the desert was the importance of an elder, a wise, holy, experienced person who could act as a teacher and guide for another. Typically, such an elder would meditate deeply on Scripture, reflect much on God in his daily experience, and learn about the depths of human nature and divine workings through his daily struggle against the destructive passions. Commonly eight destructive passions were identified, and by taking these seriously self-knowledge was advanced.[17] These elders were transparent about themselves and expected their disciples to be transparent in pouring out the thoughts of their heart. Trust was paramount.

The lives of these desert Christians were anchored in solitude, but this was not contrary to friendship. In fact, the cultivation of silence released a greater capacity for a friendship that did not depend upon trivia. Cassian observed that the desert was pervaded by a deep spirit of friendship which was made up of people being joined together in spirit rather than by being in one place. Cassian says of this indissoluble bond between friends:

> This, I say, is what is broken by no chances,
> what no interval of time or space can sever or destroy,
> and what even death itself cannot part.[18]

The Saints' Lives

There are heartwarming stories of soul friendship in *The Lives* of Celtic saints. Many are written one, two or more centuries after the life of their subject, and may read into the life of their saint insights that were current at the time of writing.

According to Muirchu's seventh century *Life*, St Patrick stayed with Bishop Germanus of Auxerre for many years and was mentored by him. With Germanus 'he learned, loved, and treasured wholeheartedly knowledge, wisdom, purity, and every benefit to soul and spirit.'[19]

Ita, after founding and establishing her monastic community at Killeedy, Ireland, set to work ministering to all about her. Her prophetic abilities, wisdom and ardent ascetic practices earned her great respect far and wide. Indeed, she became known as 'The Foster Mother of the Saints of Ireland.' Ita fostered the boy Brendan. When he asked her what three works were most pleasing to God, and what three works were most displeasing to him, Ita replied: 'The three things that please God are true faith in God with a pure heart, a simple life with a grateful spirit, and a generosity inspired by love. The three things that most displease God are a mouth that hates people, a heart harbouring resentments, and putting reliance upon wealth.' She affirmed Brendan in his desire to leave home and embark on an adventure, telling him: 'A foreign land is calling you so that you can instruct the souls of those over there.' It seems, however, that Brendan did not consult his soul friend over practical matters. For when he returned from this first voyage, somewhat disillusioned with the setbacks suffered by their boats, Ita rebuked him for not consulting her about how to make the boats. He should have built them lighter, she said.[20]

Ita was one of those experienced and spiritually sensitive soul friends who could read people even, on occasion, when they were not physically present. This gift of seeing is unlikely to grow in spiritual directors who do not make time for frequent reflection.

Samthann, Abbess of Clonbroney, asked the teenage monk Mael-Ruain if he would accept a woman as a soul friend. He blushed deeply, bowed three times to the Trinity, remained in silence, and then said 'Yes!' When Samthann learned of his reply she is reported to have said 'I think something will come of that youth.' Mael-Ruain became one of the leaders of the eighth century *Celi De* reform movement, and wrote guidelines for soul friendship in his Rule for monks: 'We regard the first year spent under our spiritual direction as a year of purifying…When you place yourself under the guidance and control of someone else you should seek out the fire which will most fiercely burn, that is, which will spare you the least.'

'We regard the first year spent under our spiritual direction as a year of purifying'

Some stories indicate the importance attached to a soul friend's role at death. When Comhganus knew that he was dying he asked Ita to visit him and lay her hands on his lips and close his mouth at the moment of death. He felt God had revealed to him that a person on whom Ita laid hands at death would be borne straight to heaven. Ita thought this was not necessary. 'You will be glorious among God's saints,' she told him, 'what do you need from me?' Comhganus replied: 'Because of what I have asked no demon will dare to come near us on our journey, or to accuse us in any way.'[21]

Kevin became Ciaran's soul friend, and when Ciaran caught the plague Kevin was sent for, but arrived after Ciaran had died and his corpse had been placed in a chapel. However, on Kevin's arrival Ciaran's spirit returned into his body, they communed together, and exchanged gifts.[22]

The Penitentials

On the continent the church developed a process for dealing with sins which was formal, public, clericalized and reserved for major sins such as murder, adultery and apostasy. This began with a confession to a (male) priest, who laid down a suitable penance, which often meant exclusion from the church for a stated period. This rehabilitation process was used only for a minority, and only once.

In Celtic lands something very different emerged. Everybody was encouraged to be part of an ongoing process which, although it might include sanctions, was to do with growth into wholeness. This process was private and confidential. Its aim was to make restitution to the wronged person in order to build responsibility and to restore the relationship between the penitent and the wronged person or community.

It invited personal dedication to overcome weaknesses for the love of God and others. *The Penitentials* were drawn up for use by clergy, but were less rigid than on the continent over whether a confessor need be ordained. We know that women continued to act as *anamcharas* (soul friends) and no doubt they were influenced to a degree by the guidance provided in the Penitentials. In the Celtic Penitentials the confessor was a friend more than a judge.

Gildas (*c* 500–570), Finnian (d 549), David (d 601), and Columbanus (*c* 543–615), among others, drew up Penitentials which were widely used. These are self evidently designed to be a means to spiritual fitness, which is why, in my book *Soulfriendship: Celtic Insights into Spiritual Mentoring* I call them 'Fitness Training Programmes.' The prescriptions are likened to medicines given by a doctor to a sick person. But the soul friend must be flexible, and discern what is appropriate for each individual.

> For this is to be carefully observed in all penance: the length of time any one remains in his faults; what learning he has received; by what passion he is assailed; how great is his strength; with what intensity of weeping he is afflicted; and with what oppression he has been driven to sin. For Almighty God who knows the hearts of all and has bestowed diverse natures will not weigh the weights of sin in an equal scale of penance...
>
> *The Penitential of Cummean*[23]

The *Tripartite St Gaul Penitential,* composed about 800, and linked with the faith community founded by Gall in Switzerland, portrays the confessor more clearly than any other Penitential as a friend who seeks the healing of the penitent:

> As often as we assign fasts to Christians who come to penance, we ourselves ought also to unite with them in fasting for one or two weeks, or as long as we are able...For no one can raise up one who is falling beneath a weight unless he bends himself that he may reach out to him his hand; and no physician can treat the wounds of the sick unless he comes in contact with the foulness.[23]

The soul friend was encouraged to be familiar with the treasure of faith and wisdom, in Scripture and in the holy teachers of the church, he was to hand on:

> These few things concerning the remedies of penance, my dearly loved brothers, according to the pronouncement of Scripture and to the opinion of very learned people, I have tried to write down, compelled by love of you.
>
> *Penitential of Finnian*[23]

Columbanus, perhaps influenced by the Celtic warrior culture from which he came, portrayed the spiritual disciplines as necessary weapons in the battle between good and evil. But he, too, likens the process to a doctor giving medicines to treat different kinds of wounds:

> [Doctors] heal wounds in one manner, sicknesses in another, festering sores in another, eye diseases in another, fractures in another, burns in another. So also should spiritual doctors treat with diverse kinds of cures the wound of souls, their sicknesses [offences], pain, ailments and infirmities. But since this gift belongs to few...let us set out even a few prescriptions according to the traditions of our elders and according to our own partial understanding, for we prophesy in part and we know in part.[24]

Current Issues

Within the Western church the role of soul friend became clericalized, and the Reformers bypassed rather than rescued it. But it never quite died out. In the Hebrides, for example, by the nineteenth century the anamchara had become a kind of midwife of the soul, who crooned songs over the friend at death. In our time, secular versions of the soul friend are reviving. Mentoring has become widespread in fields as diverse as business and sport. In an article in *The Times* of 18 March 2003 Sue Ellicott describes how on a visit to London she kept seeing advertisements for 'life coaches.' One life coach told her 'I help people turn their lives around, and make the changes that are right for them.' The idea of soul friendship appeals to many Christians who have never had a spiritual director.

This presents a challenge to the church. In our society, with its mass education (which means that all sorts of people can be soul friends regardless of place or local structure) and with its mobility and multi-choice (through electronic media and ease of travel), it is easy for anyone to find a soul friend who supports their private preferences without reference to the church or any line of accountability. Clergy sometimes fear that if members of their church get soul friends 'off the peg' the church may lose cohesion (a valid concern) or the clergy may lose control (not necessarily so valid). In the early church in Celtic lands soul friendship operated within the context of faith communities. Those who related to the network of faith communities founded by Columba, for example, would be given a soul friend who was on the staff of one of his faith communities. To have a soul friend was part of the contract of those who took vows. Others who lived in the locality would use as a soul friend someone who was in vows. Pilgrims who travelled far, keeping a rule of life linked with their parent community, would either return to their soul friend or find one who followed a similar rule.

Should pastors be the soul friend? Rarely. Certain leaders of early Celtic faith communities were soul friends to their members, but they were rooted in the disciplines of shared silence, reflection and ethos. Such soul friends developed the gift of 'seeing,' as have some of the elders in the Russian Sketes (monastic areas) of recent centuries. The Church of England currently appoints parish clergy to be managers of non-homogeneous parish units. But other clergy whose brief includes spiritual formation may be able to fulfil such a role.

Non-stipendiary and other clergy whose brief includes spiritual formation may be able to fulfil such a role

Some churches seek to address this challenge by building a form of simple soul friendship into their ongoing church life. Adrian Leighton, when Rector of several Suffolk parishes, found a soul friend for every confirmation candidate, and they remained their soul friend for the foreseeable future. Ian Silk observed that members of his Lincoln parish of St George did not embrace the more formal concept of 'spiritual direction,' but some routinely met to talk with a friend over coffee. So the church explored how to help such friends use their meetings to address deeper issues in their spiritual journey. A church in Norwich introduced some of the principles of soul friendship to the 8 to 12-year-olds, who already met as prayer triplets each week. Each agreed to pray for the other during the week, to listen, and to focus on one thing they could do to encourage the other. These experiments are one end of the spectrum of soul friendship.

At the other end are those who believe that mature Christians and churches are best served by encouraging members to have a trained soul friend. This will preferably be someone who is not part of their own church, because the agendas of the church are often part of what needs to be sifted in a soul friendship session. L'Arche communities have a spiritual parent for each of their households, and some churches invite a soul friend of the church to periodically spend time with them. Other churches invite a soul friend to join them for a season such as Lent. This approach calls for some kind of accreditation of soul friends. In our own Community of Aidan and Hilda, for example, we ask new 'explorers' to choose as a soul friend only someone who is ordained, in vows, or who has a reference from the leader of their own church.

Questions for Reflection

1 Typically soul friends, who are in short supply, meditate deeply on Scripture, reflect much on God in daily experience, and learn about human depth and divine workings through daily struggle against evil. How do you engage in these things?

2 If you are a soul friend, or seek one, how is that soul friend accountable to the wider church?

3 It is important that both soul friend and seeker are clear about what each expects of the other.

Write out what you expect from a soul friend.

Conclusion

The three chapters of this booklet consider different aspects of Celtic Christian spirituality. Because it is an holistic spirituality, the various strands naturally come together. We have seen, for example, how Ciaran was led to a particular place as a result of discussing a prophetic vision with his then soul friend, Enda. Monenna of Killeevy, on finding that a flooded river held up the work of her faith community, discerned that this was caused by a fault in one of her sisters to whom she was soul friend. She asked them all to examine their consciences, and one of them confessed that she had carried off a bunch of garlic that did not belong to the community. By putting right something that had robbed the place of its well being, this well being—though in a different physical manifestation—was restored.[25]

Creative inter-action between soul friendship and place relates also to places of resurrection. Some of Findbarr's former students sought his advice at his hermitage amid the glorious lake and woodland of Gougane Barra. They knew that their anamchara loved this place and thought of it as his place of resurrection, yet a curious and strong conviction had grown in them that this was to be their place of resurrection. How could both these things be? Findbarr, with awesome humility and clarity, told them that they had perceived aright. Their visit had helped him realize that he must move on yet once more. Somewhere else would be his place of resurrection. According to tradition (which is currently being questioned) he walked north along the river Liffy and eventually settled at his final dwelling place. This is now Cork City, and the graceful twin spires of St Findbarr's cathedral bear testimony to the importance of both soul friendship and place in Irish spirituality.

Herbert, the hermit of Derwentwater in England's Lake District, walked for days each year in order to visit his soul friend, Cuthbert. After Cuthbert became Bishop of the northern Northumbrians he visited Carlisle, and there the two soul friends met. Cuthbert discerned that he would not live to see another annual soul friend visit. Herbert wept, and implored Cuthbert to pray that they would share the same day of resurrection. So it was that, after a long illness, Herbert in Derwentwater, died on 20 March 687, as did Cuthbert on Farne Island. The themes of intercession, prophecy, soul friendship and place interleave in this liminal event.

Earlier in his life Cuthbert had been extremely busy, first as a missionary based at Melrose, and then as prior of the mission monastery at Lindisfarne. Yet it was when he retired to the solitude of Farne Island that his role as soul friend came to the fore. Bede observed:

> Now Cuthbert had great numbers of people coming to him not just from Lindisfarne but even from the remote parts of Britain. They confessed their sins, confided in him about their temptations and laid open to him the common troubles of humanity they were labouring under—all in the hope of gaining consolation from so holy a man. They were not disappointed. No one left unconsoled; no one had to carry back the burdens he came with. Spirits that were chilled with sadness he could warm back to hope again with a pious word. Those beset with worry he brought back to thoughts of the joys of Heaven… To those beset with temptation he would skilfully disclose all the wiles of the devil, explaining that a soul lacking in love for God or people is easily caught in the devil's nets, while one that is strong in faith can, with God's grace, brush them aside like so many spider's webs.[26]

Some eleven years after Cuthbert's death a major event took place—the Lindisfarne Gospels were dedicated in honour of God and St Cuthbert. Recent scholarly opinion is that these Gospels made a statement, and were a kind of first 'manifesto' of the English Church. Hitherto, the northern English churches had been led by the Irish, and the southern English churches by Romans. Here was the first major 'leader product' that was Anglo-Saxon in its origin and mission statement. It is certain that consultation took place with other major centres of the Anglo-Saxon church in Northumbria, such as Jarrow and Hexham. Although most of the artwork in these exquisite volumes comprises the standard illustrations one would expect in any such illuminated Gospels, three were particular to the Lindisfarne Gospels. These may be taken to represent the typical spirituality of St Cuthbert and the emerging English church.

They were the Beatitudes, the Lost Son Parable and the Temptations of Jesus. The Beatitudes, or 'Beautiful Attitudes,' speak of the simplicity and vulnerability of the original faith and of its contemporary monastic expression. The Lost Son Parable speaks of the compassion and hospitality at the heart of God which is meant also to be at the heart of Christ's church. The Temptations speak of the reality of spiritual struggle at both a natural and supernatural level. Only in the context of ceaseless prayer can these flowers of beautiful attitudes and hospitality flourish.

This is our birthright and it is also God's call to us—to restore to a church that is bound by bureaucracy the simplicity of Jesus' way, to establish welcoming, holy presence at the heart of every community in which friendship and spiritual formation are the norm, and to overcome the 'light half-belief in casual creeds' with a ceaseless rhythm of prayer and praise.

This is our birthright and it is also God's call to us

This book introduces just a few themes of Celtic Christianity. My first book, *Exploring Celtic Spirituality*,[27] examined twenty-two themes. Following the publication of an early edition a Cambridge physicist concluded that these provided the church's agenda for the next thirty years. The three themes of this booklet—rhythm, roots and relationship—are central to the story of the garden of Eden (Genesis 2). Human beings walk in rhythm with God, in a sacred place and in transparent fellowship. This ageless aspiration need not be a mere dream. For Christians in our own land in the early centuries after Christ made heroic efforts to make these things a reality in their homes, churches and neighbourhoods. We, too, must do the same.

Resources for the Practical Application of the Themes of This Book

Place

Volume Three of the author's four volume series *The Celtic Prayer Book*, provisionally entitled *Healing the Land: Sacraments and Special Services* (Kevin Mayhew, 2003)

Healing Wounded History: Reconciling Peoples and Healing Places by Russ Parker (DLT, 2001)

Healing Wounded History: The Workbook by Michael Mitton and Russ Parker (DLT, 2001)

Soul Friendship

These three books by the author are useful tools for the soul friend:

Soulfriendship: Celtic Insights Into Spiritual Mentoring (Hodders, 1999) Explores practical guidelines, pitfalls and skills of soul friendship.

Before We Say Goodbye: Preparing for a Good Death (HarperCollins, 2001) Offers a practical and reassuring resource both for preparing for our own deaths and for ministering to the dying.

Spiritual Fitness (Zondervan, 2003) A year's training programme.

Notes

1   Oliver Davies, *Celtic Spirituality* (Classics of Western Spirituality, Paulist Press, 1999) p 3.

2   Ian Bradley, in *Columba: Pilgrim and Penitent* (Wild Goose Publications, 1997).

3   Philip Newell, in *Celtic Benediction* (Canterbury Press, 2000) Preface.

4   David Adam, *The Eye of the Eagle* (SPCK, 1990) p 10.

5   Ian Bradley, *Celtic Christianity: Making Myths and Chasing Dreams* (Edinburgh University Press, 1999).

6   John O'Donohue, *Anamcara: Spiritual Wisdom from the Celtic World* (Bantam, 1997) p 42.

7   Gildas, *The Ruin of Britain* (Phillimore, 1978) p 19.

8   Bede, *The Eccesiastical History of the English People,* Book 1, Chapter 18 (OUP, 1994) p 32.

9   T S Eliot, *Murder in the Cathedral* (Faber and Faber, 1938) page 87.

10 Recorded in Whitley Stokes (trans), *Lives of Saints from The Book of Lismore* (Llanerch reprint 1995) p 219.

11 *The Life of St Darerca, or Moninna* in Liam De Paor, *Saint Patrick's World* (Four Courts Press, 1993) p 291.

12 Bede, *The Eccesiastical History of the English People* Book 3 Chapter 23 (OUP, 1994) p 148.

13 John O'Donohue, *Anamcara: Spiritual Wisdom from the Celtic World* (Bantam, 1997) p 124.

14 Aelred, *Life of Ninian* in *Two Celtic Saints* (Llanerch, 1989) ch 7, p 16.

15 Community of Aidan and Hilda, *The Celtic Prayer Book*, Volume Three: *Healing the Land: Sacraments and Special Services* (Kevin Mayhew, 2003).

16 Many of these *Lives* were written one or two centuries after the death of the saint. *The Oxford Dictionary of Saints* (OUP, 1999) refers to the earliest sources available for most of the notable Celtic saints.

17 The eight destructive passions are gluttony, avarice, rage, self-pity, lust, slackness, vanity, pride. See Simpson, Ray, *Soulfriendship: Celtic Insights Into Spiritual Mentoring* (Hodder & Stoughton, 1999) pp 131–138.

18 John Cassian, *Conferences* 16 ch 3 translated in P Schaff and H Wace (eds) *A Select Library of Nicene and Post-Nicene Fathers of the Christian Church* (Grand Rapids: William B Eerdmans).

19 Muirchu, *Life of St Patrick,* in Liam De Paor, *Saint Patrick's World* (Four Courts Press, 1993) p 178.

20 See *The Life of Brenainn* in Whitley Stokes (trans), *Lives of Saints in the Book of Lismore* (Llanerch, 1995) pp 248–261.

21 *Life of Ita* in C Plummer (ed), *Vitae Sanctorum Hiberniae* (2 vols 1968) pp 116–130.

22 *Life of Ciaran* in Whitley Stokes (trans), *Lives of Saints in the Book of Lismore* (Llanerch, 1995) p 278.

23 As quoted in Edward C Sellner, *The Celtic Soul Friend* (Ave Maria Press, 2002) pp 89–193.

24 G S M Walker, *Sancti Columbani Opera* (Dublin Institute for Advanced Studies, 1070) Penitential p 173.

25 *The Life of St Darerca, or Moninna* in Liam De Paor, *Saint Patrick's World* (Four Courts Press, 1993) p 284.

26 Bede, *Life of Cuthbert* 22 in *The Age of Bede* (Penguin, 1985) p 71.

27 A new, revised edition of Ray Simpson, *Exploring Celtic Spirituality: Historic Roots for Our Future* is to be published with a study guide by Kevin Mayhew 2003/4.